HHB

Riverborne

A Mississippi Requiem

Poems by

Peter Neil Carroll

𝓗𝓗𝓑

Higganum Hill Books : Higganum, Connecticut

First Edition
First Printing September 1, 2008

Higganum Hill Books
P.O. Box 666, Higganum, CT 06441
Phone (860) 345-4103
Email: rcdebold@mindspring.com

Cover image: *Our Banner in the Sky*, Frederick Church 1861.
Frontispiece: *Bound Down the River*, Currier and Ives 1870.
Author photograph by Jeannette Ferrary, ©2007, used by permission.

Library of Congress Control Number: 2007044090
ISBN13: 978-0-9776556-9-4

Library of Congress Cataloging-in-Publication Data

Carroll, Peter N.
  Riverborne : a Mississippi requiem : poems / by Peter Neil Carroll. -- 1st ed.
    p. cm.
  ISBN-13: 978-0-9776556-9-4 (alk. paper)
  1. Mississippi River--Poetry. I. Title.
  PS3603.A7748R58 2008
  811'.6--dc22

                                        2007044090

Independent Publishers Group distributes Higganum Hill Books.
Phone: (800) 888-4741   www.ipgbook.com
Printed in the United States of America.

Dedication

For Jeannette

Acknowledgements

The Waverly Poets of Palo Alto were the first to hear some of these poems, and for their encouragement I thank in particular Charlotte Muse, Palmer Pinney, Elaine McCreight, and Beth Mills. Richard Silberg and Joyce Jenkins of Poetry Flash gave good editorial advice. Jayne Kos and the Not Yet Dead Poets Society provided an early forum. John T. Daniel, long a source of inspiration and laughter, focused the final phase of revision. With undiminished trust, Michael Batinski supported the project from start to finish. Without Jeannette Ferrary, none of it would make any sense.

Author's Note: All italicized words come from the writings of Mark Twain. References appear in the Endnotes.

Contents

1

1
April

I'd Stood On That Cold Bridge, 1972

in Minneapolis,

shadowed the careless current, stroked
the iron rail that lured release. Jump
and everything would cease,
even hard words that pursued me

until all thought
joined the river.

I didn't jump
healed by drier means and lived alone
for temptation, desire,
looked for my chance
to follow the river's hip-swiveling mystery
down to the lowest ripples.

My fugitive friend, Jim, suddenly free,
his wife gone, free but not more happy;
we cut pocket-knife oaths to take
the living stream down to the bronze tail
on General Jackson's horse
in New Orleans.

Call me Huck Finn, I declared;
making me Nig Jim?, he asked with a slouch.

This Time, 2005

The river this time meant second sight,

> *recognized him at once...old and white-headed...*
> *the boy of fifteen*

We'd see what Jim and I saw
thirty years before the millennium,
two men, 29, divorced,
crazy with freedom.

Seeing what we'd seen completely gone:

gone the way a slender birch tilts
to the running current, slips roots, thrashes,
drowns;

gone as a splintery oak thickens
its limbs into unrecognizable age;

gone the way two men get bleached
under fast moving suns, rained upon, lose
the shade of hair, their speed.

> *made a trumpet of his hands*
> *at my ear...in a yell like a foghorn –*

First time, spirited boys laughed
at everything unfamiliar; this time
curious but wary, scenting the past
in its strange shapes.

> *"Same damned fools, Sam!"*

What We Talked About First, 2005

                    Minneapolis
Three decades later,
how little we remembered that first hasty trip:
the day after Christmas, Nixon in the White House
gas 29 cents, maroon Ford Galaxy blasting
against gray winds, rushed to beat a blizzard,
roadside spittled with puzzling white frosts

until we saw it was cotton, tall chocolate women
stooped over the crop, inching along,
a catch-bag trails their path,
skinny dog trails the bag, kids trail the dog.

Stopped at Sambo's café, we played at stuttering,
shuffling as if chains bound our ankles;
cracked jokes about Mississippi senators

     but Jim said it would fetch bad luck

and abruptly we quit kidding, skipped breakfast,
dragged out, gravel snapping the hind wheels,
past a fast southbound freight tracking the Gulf port,
watched the slow river stroke toward New Orleans.

Divorced, feeling free, we caught
Shreveport country & western on the AM dial,
thought mostly of eat, sleep, then
a stroll in the Quarter, red beans and rice,
shots of Bourbon, Dixieland, maybe a barfly
for the night, maybe the blues –
Jim wrinkles a lip, asks: "Is grits plural?"

The View Downstream, 2005

The first night:
starlight in a warm Minnesota sky,
whispery river below the bridge,
a cream-colored froth reflects city lights,
slides toward a delicate bend;

the west-bank bluff stretches,
shifts the current eastward, portside,
as a hand presses against the dancer's waist
draws the lover away, then back in close embrace,
a bump, a glance.

The bend blocks the view, arouses:
What lies beyond the shore's thigh?
Does the high breeze cool the beach?
What's on this side of the night?

> *the "point" above the town,*
> *and the "point" below,*
> *bounding the river-glimpse. . .*
> *still and brilliant and lonely*

Riverside glistens, combed green;
a softball field, boys gather gloves and jackets,
walk together after the game;
we parallel their path on the bridged height,
approach tall branches of bare trees
dressed with castaway pairs of gym shoes,
a girl's brassiere, strange ritual of wintered students.

"Here," I said to Jim, "Here's where we start."

Coveting The Shore

Prescott, Wisconsin,

Below the iron railroad bridge,
the icy-clear St. Croix dissolves
into the Mississippi like spoonfuls of sugar in coffee.

Yellow real estate signs, prolific as dandelions,
announce refurbished Victorians, luxury condos;
the Antique Mall promotes "collectibles,"
deer heads from waterfront taxidermists.

> *The city. . .greatly changed,*
> *but it did not seem so*
> *. . .can't persuade a new thing*
> *to look new*

An old timer, his laced lady caught in a flood
of tourists, grumbles about Minnesotans mooring motorboats
at upscale restaurants, buying out the town.

High on Dakota Hill, a red spire looms, Jim steers
toward the steepled overlook. Knights of Columbus
have planted a stony abstract mother and child,
shaped like crooked-neck zucchini, one wombs
the other:

> "In loving memory of God's unborn,
> denied the precious right to life."

The old-ways religion resists
invading cosmopolitans:
culture war's coming to Prescott.

Against the Skyline

Diamond Bluff, Wisconsin

Winter-thin trees against the gray skyline,
not a route marker in half hour's wandering;
Jim and I, city boys, circle woodsy roads,
disoriented –
but not for long:

Before us,
a cinder block cathedral,
freshly painted, bright lavender

BORDER LOUNGE

"Well, well," Jim studies the billboard

EXOTIC DANCERS

I know what we'd do thirty years back.
Jim also knows:

"Let's not go there."

What They Talk About On Saturday Afternoon

Lake Pepin, Wisconsin

apple roasting. . .sizzling on a hearth. . . .
sugar. . .a drench of cream. . .

In the chrome café perched above
frayed cabins on stilts, the talkative chef's
a software prodigy turned sandwich-maker,
shows a flair for minced ginger, peanut sauce.

Late sun leans against the Minnesota bluff
across the river, orange streaks skim
the current, snagged islands float offshore,
an outboard motor barks.

Entering loudly, a bundled mother, stout daughter
order April's first burgundy-cherry rum,
double scoops on sugar cones,
plunk down on swivel stools,
chat about readying rooms for summer tourists,
end of the drought: "Not much work lately,"
thick Swede lilt; "we'll start tomorrow."

Seasoned woman, wallet in hand,
        approaches the counter boy:
                "How much money should I take out?"
        asks her cautious voice
                about to cast the winter's hoard to spring.

At The Edge of Town

near Maiden Rock, Wisconsin

We-no-na ran to its summit
. . .upbraided her parents. . .
their cruelty. . .threw herself
from the precipice.

She was a good deal jarred up
and jolted: but she got herself together
and disappeared.

"Welcome Bikers – It's Miller Time"

Choppers at Ole's happy time saloon line the front yard
like World War II bombers, silvered, their eager pilots
beery, as in movies with widows-to-be scream-singing

"Roll Out The Barrel"

One sun-glassed cyclist's lettered leather jacket:

IF YOU CAN READ THIS
THE BITCH FELL OFF

"Fell or jumped?" cracks Jim;
he knows about women
who leave men in a hurry,
the bluff landscape of Lovers' Leaps,
how women descend,
                              fallen, felled.

The biker in dark goggles gooses the throttle,
woman behind him clutches leathered biceps,
sees the one good road out of town.
Her dream; his fear; her insistence; his fury.

My Grandpa Was Two

Trempealeau, Wisconsin

Uphill block of red-brick buildings,
open for waterside business, 1888,
year my grandpa turned two;
grain merchants now gone,
The Woodmen's Society,
old sawbones barber, gone;
above the river, an oblong plaque
badges the arched doorways.

Makes me remember the immigrant glazier,
my Grampa, who windowed such buildings:
He'd stand, one black boot braced
on the highest rung,
one hung in space,
instep balancing a light of glass
about to enter the frame; he'd hum
a gravelly tune, dance his body weight,
heave big shoulders, push hard,
then tap a tin dart into the sash.

Before my eyes the building rises
as two gentlemen pass behind me;
one points his cane,
saying to his spry mate,
"My Daddy used to own that site" –
and the workers who sang, my grandpa,
as if someone's kicked the ladder from under their feet,
drop from the scaffold,
vanish from a small town's past.

The Only Trouble

La Crosse

A choice town,
electric-lighted streets. . .buildings. . .stately
says Mr. Clemens' nostalgia guide,
his steamboat stopped for an hour's visit in the rain.

Hungry, Jim and I deploy downtown,
streets dark, stately doorways deserted,
except for twilight men tippling from paper sacks.
Pink neon flashes: enchiladas, rice and beans;
nothing's open. Riverside cafes show
yellow-eyed bass, catfish dusted with cornmeal,
closed for vacation.

We find, finally, "Family Fare": but the "fresh fish"
comes ice-cored; I question the menu:
"it *was* fresh," swears the gum popping waitress,
"when they caught it." Beans mush, mash lumped;
kids in the next booth order Suicide Pop, all-flavor swill,
made us reminisce about our previous great meals –

Eight white donuts and a beer for lunch;
canned ravioli cooked in the can
until patties rose above the hot rim,
we plucked them like Italian candies,
dreamed all night on bad stomachs.

"Wisconsin's the second most obese state," brags
the waitress at All-You-Can-Eat Brunch down river:
grim farmers limp on torn joints, bellies bulging
over fabric belts, devour powdered pancakes,
scrambles, double linked sausage, bacon and beans,
deep fried spuds, apple pie and coffee.

11

I'm glutted, but Jim scarfs a dish of runny eggs and ham,
declares, "the only trouble here" –
one hand pats his stomach, one grips the fork –
"food here tastes pretty damn good."

Jim Finds Religion

on the Iowa bluffs

Raised on evangelical sermons, now Jim attends
Quaker meetings, gives him an eye for spiritual irony,
second-hand crucifixes, anomalous yard signs:

JESUS SAVES

JACKPOT PRIZES!

THOU SHALT NOT

Hills rise on the western edge,
Mississippi plunges through a treed gorge;
first green buds sprout from every limb,
sun at twelve o'clock,
high country gnarled by spring runs.
Jim's still grumbling: "I know those people.
Where I live they're taking over the schools."

A blood-mouthed hawk suddenly soars
from his prey on the roadside
into the 360-degree heavenly bowl.
He stops mid-sentence.
We're overcome by abundant hills, tall silos;
through a yard-gate, a colt sucks teat,
the farm appears as a child's colored picture:
white-washed fences, emerald field,
royal-blue sky summons a prayer,

divinity Jim can't resist; he drives
down a pebbled lane,
drops through dark woods,
long pines blanket the light,
across a wood-bridged brook to the river's edge,
abandoned,

but for us, the river; a birdsong choir
whistles the spring gospel;
green pollen paints the shore-bound roots,
birds dance in bare branches, twitching sounds
broken by mid-river ducks blowing trombones.

A yellow stone sunk in river mud conjures gold,
I palm sweet water into my mouth,
Jim studies the trees, his mouth moves silently

> *tranquil and reposeful as dreamland. . .*
> *nothing this-worldly about. . – nothing*
> *to hang a fret or a worry. . .*

Observed, he drops the trance,
delivers his sermon:
"They have no idea what is sacred."

Sunday at the Riverside

Guttenberg, Iowa

Silence is audible, until Ingram's Towboat motor starts
to cough, jolts awake the suited man
on a riverside bench; he glares at the harsh engine
shoving a herd of barges downstream,
around the jutting point.

What remains is Sunday afternoon, springtime
on the pier, boys fish, break into laughter,
an old timer grinds a reel, his pulls attract attention
but the line suddenly falls slack.

The running river speaks in signs, spills a low wave
to shore, startles a bare-armed mother spoon-feeding
her baby on the grass. Slow sun scorches
the torpid air, the wakened man lifts
a staticky radio to his ear,
catches the first pitch from St. Louis.

Replenish the Earth

South of North Buena Vista

One Iowa field pushes two thousand bushels of corn,
another feeds a moving herd of cows;
two wayward horses consume
an untended haystack. The landlord's rich,
reaps millions from machines:
seeders, threshers, ploughs, pumps, tractors.

Flush times, the land grows big houses;
faux deer on green lawns sniff the pruned trees,
marble rabbits pursue Easter eggs. In asphalt driveways,
basketball hoops await high school students;
but Jim reports he's seen only white kids
since two black teenagers dribbled in an unlit schoolyard
way back in La Crosse. After all, says Jim,
why should the fat soil give a damn
about racial integration?

A yellow Dead End signals, Jim hits
the brake, crosses the gravel road
to a doddering white-framed church
on a rise, relic of evangelists;
a rickety rail fence outlines a garden of weeds,
sunken rectangles, weather-bleached gravestones

JACKSON, CRAWFORD, THOMASES

Soundless but for a sudden whiplash,
the rising wind snaps the flag on a high steel pole;
cat-like cries respond,
the church door scrapes on a rusted hinge.

> *it might be the spirits*
> *of the dead complaining*
> *at being disturbed*

We Talk Of Our Fathers

driving to Dubuque,

who were never older than we are.
Fatherless boys,
bred by men who moved on,
leaving our fathers
with only what lay under skin:
steel backs, an ear for pitch,
bodies that would explode
into enormous fits of laughter
at being their own fathers

and ours. Big men, they earned
their bread, hoped for a break;
never understood
the rules of the game,
that there was a game.
A brooding rage loomed

over their little boys,
the smoke they blew
frightening. Our fathers envied us,
eventually, had meant no harm,
but we parented our own boys

more gently. Our sons,
already men with boys and girls –
                such speed, Jim, such distance:
your Cossack grandpa sword-slashing my Litvak Jews;
today we shipped river postcards to four grandchildren.

Now we sing in two voices:

lyrics of those hard-worked fathers
struggling to sink roots in concrete streets;
our grandchildren's songs of Sesame Street,

the letter K, say, for a kiss,
the number 2 for their lips;

we grasp hands our fathers never held.

Visitation Rites

Dubuque, Iowa

Thickening clouds infuse
a sour smell of afternoon rain,
the riverfront slumbers.
A flashy casino barker hustles trade.
Jim picks a drab bar,
orders coffee for a second wind.

Above dark tables in hardwood booths,
St. Louis Redbirds flicker in late innings;
Jim recalls stark corners
with his son, lonely Illinois Sundays
on the outskirts of town:
bowling alleys closed, movies screened,
fed full with Macs or Whoppers,
strawberry shakes, hours still to the kid's curfew.

Weekend dads, we entertained
our consequences, mother-raised boys
bewildered, bored; we filled
the void telling tales:
my trickstered youth, momentous ball fields,
history's amazing Friday, Kennedy killed,
or sieging '68 Chicago, wounded friends at Kent State.

We told of known outlaws, the revolution;
at a peace parade, a motorist yelled
"Traitors! Traitors!"
my boy petrified, Jim's kid promises
"won't tell Mom," first time
Jim realized his son understood:
cheery thought in bleak Dubuque.

19

A Digression To Grant's House

Galena, Illinois

Jim opens the screen door:
horse-hair rocker idles in the front room,
abandoned kettles squat
on the cold stove, lead-lined tub
holds dusty dishes.
Creaky stairs lead to the bedrooms,
the General's black linen suit, shapeless
as spirit, hangs in the bare closet.

Galena (a parenthesis
for not-yet General U.S. Grant,
failed soldier-farmer-sales clerk,
hands strapped to his father's harness shop,
then catapulted through carnage
into glory –

Shiloh, Vicksburg:

> *ground-shaking thunder-crashes. . .*
> *bombshells. . .scream and crash. . .*

Chattanooga, The Wilderness, Appomattox

Back home the hero, a rose-petal parade,
city fathers gifted the red brick house on a hillside.

> Since Grant has whipped the Rebel Lee
> And opened trade from sea to sea
> Our goods in price must soon advance
> Then don't neglect the present chance
> To call on GRANT. . .

20

Strangers rushed him for handshakes,
his autograph.

The great man shrugged,
yearned for a busy life,
left town forever,
closed the parenthesis).

I've Been Thinking, Says Jim

South of Healey, Iowa

Slow drizzle brushes
the rolling Iowa bluffs,
cows cluster beneath budded leaves.

Across the bridge over swollen Spruce Creek,
damp light-gray sky
blossoms with song, I whistle
to the birds.

"I've been thinking,"
Jim says, pauses a moment,
out drops the news,
"about retiring."

Thoughts race back
the shy boy ambitious to teach history:
how men bowed before majesty;
pioneers roasted buffalo humps;
re-breathing buried voices,
forty years he's lectured,

retiring? Sees my surprise,
starts to say…stops.
I know why he's embarrassed:
for years we've joked about the idle prospect,
old men raising beers, golf sticks, baggy hind quarters.

His eyes shrink in dull light.
look away to the nearest woolly-green island.

"What about history?" I plead.
"Whose history?" he snaps.

Tell the River

(Ten minutes later)

Pretend the River's your student, Jim.

Explain the French influence
    the English, Spanish
    American Indian
    African American
    Yankee, Dixieland

Talk about Jefferson, the Louisiana Purchase.

Tell the river about everyone
who would own it.

Three Days Down River

               through Bellevue, Clinton,
               the Quad cities.

The river minds her business:
wheat, oats, rye ride elevators
into open-mouthed boats;

where glaciers stopped,
the landscape flattens,
river bluffs shrink;
men with chains parceled the earth
into checkerboard farms,
excavated Davenport's gravel pits:
"Look Out For Blowing Dust!" the quarry sign warns;

 and just when machines nearly bury the river,
a horn blasts three times--
             LOOK, LOOK, LOOK –
                   and who's here
but the Ingram Towboat,
twenty-two hours south from Guttenberg,
still shoving six barges downstream at LeClair.

Another mile, and the shoreline flares
into redbuds, pink dogwood, flowering,
apple, peach, mulberry, yellow forsythia;
the topsoil gleams like onyx in rainlight;
the beauty of the beauty parlor sign:

       THIS LITTLE TOWN IS HEAVEN TO US,
       PLEASE DON'T DRIVE LIKE HELL

We stick to the blacktop highway, Burlington, Fort Madison
(first Stars & Stripes 1803), Keokuk, past Twain's print shop;
nothing's so pretty as blurred memory.

We catch the river's next bridge,
        cross over her rolling belly
               just for the tickle she gives.

We Pause To Consider The Meaning of Life

Quincy, Illinois

Spring-bathed Adams County shouts greetings:

LIFE IS GOOD

meaning, this good-for-nothing-to-do city's
      the best place
            for a breather, time to consider
                Twain's daunting
                        destiny question:

Mamma, what's it all for?

For two weary travelers,
      life's logic never-the-less clear:

Life's for our goods: house auto bed tables books
laptops DVDs Visa ATM
two-door icebox, clouds of laundry,
      digital clocks running;

For our immaterials: wife kids grandchildren a hopeless
romance ambition humor sweet retirement, awareness
      the clocks running;

For two guys who've explored Alaska, lobstered Maine,
California beaches, Kansas in a blizzard, Detroit, New Harmony,
Lincoln's Springfield, Minneapolis in winter, holy St. Paul,
the Mississippi River,
           flowing;

For the nonsense we've shared: spiraling footballs;
losing a suitcase at the airport; chiseling a porcelain
toilet bowl hole; the unopened Scotch bottle crash,
straining liquored sponges from waxed floor; Tampax

you find in my New Orleans baggage; our enemies list.

Mamma, what's it all for?

For talking shop: history, memory.
For considering insoluble problems.
For proposing insoluble solutions.

For our telepathic efficiencies; entering sentences
mid-stream, where the water's most pure, effluent,
and we speak in metaphors about what's real, but runs
before our eyes.

For as time rushes,
we'll never be here again, neither
giddy boys on a spree, nor
weathered men measuring
what little we have left.

Hazy Day, Just After Sunrise

Hannibal, Missouri

Jim patrols past tourist shops,
pushes open a café door,
deep fries choke the air,
mustachioed workers
puff breakfast cigars.

We browse Christian flyers
taped to the counter,
gung-ho for the troops in Iraq,
assorted patriot clamor;
we hear Twain grumble and sigh.

Jim rolls his eyes,
hold our opinions until outside,
then stroll Twain's tourist route,
"America's Home Town":
the village he revisited

> *new houses – saw. . .plainly enough*
> *– but. . ..through. . .solid bricks and mortar. . .*
> *saw the vanished houses. . .formerly stood there*
> *with perfect distinctness*

Mark Twain Museum,
Mark Twain Hotel,
The Mark Twain Clopper
The Mark Twain Museum Annex,
Clemens Justice of the Peace Office,
Mark Twain's Boyhood Home,
the anchored red, white, & blue
sidewheeling Mississippi steamboat
red-lettered capitals,

MARK TWAIN

– whole town's rehabilitated, restored,
white-washed, gentrified, facsimiled,
leased, ticketed, priced

and then Jim spots real trouble in very fine print

THIS PARK MONITORED BY VIDEO SURVEILLANCE

River Watching

Glascock's Landing, Hannibal

A black-tailed shore bird sails above the river bank,
the white-haired man lifts a palm to shade his brow,
watches the bird descend onto an upstretched branch
of a drifting still-green willow tree.

Bird rides the willow as the current spins into eddies,
pulling round, round, like a treading swimmer,
then bursts downstream,
past the jutting land point that shutters the old man's view.

His eyes lift to the mid-river islands, wild with birdsong,
and then eastward into Illinois, searches
two miles, maybe three,
until the oblique riverbend closes the light.

Here Twain began to see, in bits of bark and leaf, clumps of lawn,
floating picket boards, a front door unhinged, diamond-shaped window
lighting the ghostly undertow, pine-shingled roof gored by an apple lim
uprooted rooms, treasure in ransacked drawers, pirates, a human corpse

Fantasies followed the floods: he read his future in hieroglyphics
printed on rippling waters, scribbles of debris; imagined a fortune,
cultivated ambition, humor for flawed authority;
the stymied boy schemed.

Hannibal's north bluff summons us up Cardiff Hill,
risky steps for aging men who stumble on the path, rising
as light breaks the leafy canopy.

From the summit, the Illinois shore reaches into yellow-green hills,
rumpled islands float like cushions lost in a storm.
Still the riverbend stops the eye; upward we climb,
more light enters but the stubborn cape remains opaque:
too damn old to scale a tree!

Below sleeps Twain's snug village, criss-cross of streets,
brick sidewalks, white clapboard houses, small shops,
swinging signs creaked in the wind,
all circled by hills *in a half-moon curve,*
the stone-paved landing quiet, the town in a doze.

Twice daily, the gaudy steamboat roars, steam valves screech,
sailors shout, the whole world arrives – and then
in a dime's time, upstream or down,
she's gone, the river resumes.

Easy to imagine boys craving adventure,
the white-haired man returning,
shades his brow, measures the distance;
two old men come to dream across the mile-wide water.

We Run Into Two Boys

                              below Cardiff Hill,

Interlocked as bronze lovers,
they play on the eternal playing field,
slingshot in one boy's pocket, corncob pipe
in the other's,

destined: to be pirates, explorers, pilots,
more likely casualties of the coming civil war.

> *comrades and yet*
> *not comrades; color*
> *and condition interposed*
> *a subtle line*

Tom and Huck: "fine boys," we hear a tourist say.
"Fine white boys," mutters Jim,
his namesake left off the squad.

Wrenched From Hannibal

"St. Louey" bound,
vague general knowledge of its wonders;

Dawdling at the backside of Huck's riverbend bluff, eager to run
south, but held as the past holds a tune,
watch the waters speed south; we await
our spinning green-willow tree, bird-sailor aboard, but she doesn't show;
the river now a cold stripe between wooded banks.

We climb Victor's Point, view the inland valley, imbibe
ploughed aroma; fields shimmer as mirrored lakes,
red-bud in leaf; white barns, silver silos bob like sailboats
moored to earth. Behind us the full river surges.

Surrender dears, she demands: this lovely body's swimming to the big-
time town.

We follow along, rush past lonely villages,
colorless barns, acres of beef; two short-haired boys in a front yard wave
at our car;
and then the river twists around a bend, shows skin, her art:
for who's that rolling on fast dark waters,
48 hours south of Guttenberg, dancing in sunlight,
but the trusty Ingram Towboat, six barges pointed to St. Louis.

domes and steeples. . .
blossom of peach trees in city garden. . .
umbrella of black smoke

We catch up above Clarksville, Lock & Dam No. 24,
huge steel gates, bolts bang the brown tide to a stop
like grabbing a big-hipped swimmer,
shoving her into a wet loony-bin, her soprano pleas
taken for a joke: Hold still, sister!
her whimper, the undertow rubs against the steel cage,

chains run along her flanks, grind, rattle, screams of confinement;
her ordeal an hour before a square-jawed bailsman sets the corpus free.

St. Louis woman shakes her hair,
slips on a silk chemise,
Jim and I pursue the curling fingers.

Riverfront Silence

St. Louis, Missouri

The night we land the Cardinals play Houston under the lights,
streets near empty, corner hustlers scalp late fans;
weary sales clerks await the fumed buses, downtown streets pull up
the blankets, bedtime at dusk.

The riverfront's Memorial Gateway Arch
(six hundred thirty foot city logo)
belittles the Mississippi. The nation's vein runs north to south,
but the metallic curve twists history's axis, pulls
the eye westerly to placards of pioneer fables,
Lewis & Clark rising to the Rockies, going coastal,
Conestoga trails, transcontinental rail, the interstate;
the water maiden's left behind.

> *pavements. . .bad;*
> *sidewalks. . .out of repair;*
> *struggling throngs of men,. . .*
> *mountains of freight . . .gone*

The river's shrunk, concrete defeats fluidity,
wharves bare, nowhere to jump aboard,
even the water birds strut on dry land.

We lost her, says Jim.

2

August

Coming Back Into The Country

Below St. Louis

Landing after dawn at Lambert Field,
airport packed, sudden screams
two black fighter jets race down the runway

shudder the walls, panic turns my stomach
– the country's still at war. I rush
for an exit, find Jim behind the wheel.

The air-conditioned Chrysler's running.
In minutes we reach another landscape,
hushed, unmoving.

A sullen heat descends, airless;
the distant river, a crescent,
drifts blue between yellow hills.

Cornfields tawny, drought-
parched, spring dreams
dissolved, powder in the palm.

The land is hard, flat
as the vanished riverbed;
still, the cool waters

are flowing south –
to refresh the seeds
or confirm despair?

Imaginary River

Kaskaskia, Illinois

Almost-abandoned, this French settlement,
La Grande Rue fronts an imaginary river,
the locked church
preserves the Liberty Bell
of the West, gift of Louis XV
to five hundred pious colonists,

awakened one morning to find
a colossal theft –
the mud-brown river gone!
Devious upstream waters
left the town high and dry.

Corn sunbathes on city lots,
a solitary forager bolts aloft,
wings eastward
through dense yellow heat,
hoping for a cloud that chimes.

The Missing River

Ste. Genevieve County, Missouri

We follow the fugitive bird along farmed, scraggly hills;
weathered houses, trailers, outbuildings cluster
as almost-towns.

On Sugar Bottom Road we seek the missing Mississippi,
the river's there all right, its the reason
no roads parallel the shore,
but always a farmer's fence,
limestone shippers' machine, electric power plant,
interrupts the crow's route.

The levee at Cape Girardeau suddenly opens the vista:
towboat low in the water, motor drumming,
nudges six scows loaded with white rock downstream;
the quiet river sweeps past
the struggling vessel

until the noisy bang, clunk, and grind
of a rocking northbound freight
breaks into the picture,
robs the town of everything,
but memory.

Outskirts

Thebes, Illinois

We enter the hilltop village,
easily rememberable, says Twain,
overlooks *the Great Chain of sunken rocks*
admirably arranged to capture and kill
steamboats on bad nights.

Pioneers erected the yellow
Greek Revival Court House,
now the outskirts of importance;
here fugitive slaves
heard the gavel's thud,
slumped when heavy cell doors locked.

Our response, shock, silence. Quick
we descend to the abandoned waterfront;
pier timbers rise into air like black cactus,
a fifty foot sand bar stretches the beach.

Mississippi, moving fast, mirrors
a leaden sky. We're still shaken,
the slave monument hovering on the hillside,
startled when a fresh-painted stern-wheeler
sails a deck of gamblers toward southern casinos.

Soon we hear approaching chuffs of a scow,
rugged engine, barges high with red sand;
Jim reads the name on her bow – the Ingram Towboat!
The prow cuts through, wake washing to shore,
hurries away from the stone relic behind us.

Ancient Wisdom

Cairo, Illinois

Brisk town, substantially built,
reports the steamboat pilot.

Grim town, mean, insists Jim,
leading me along steamy streets,
temperature over 100°:
a bare-chested man spraying bug poison
from a rubber hose, his wife, three kids watch,
squat outside the uncooled trailer;
two corner boys, cigarettes dangle in thin lips,
stare defiantly.

On her daddy's porch, a young grandmother
recalls child summers,
splash-sounds, screeches from the public pool,
no black kids allowed;
instead, the stubborn mayor buried the pool.
At the movies, she sat in Nigger Heaven
until fires extinguished the feral downtown.

Brick rubble fouls the sidewalks,
plywood replaces showroom glass.
Across town a shady Mansion Row
survives on red-brick streets,
permits gardeners, cooks, maids during daylight;
other blacks understand not to parade white streets:
the grandmother explains this ancient wisdom.

Rather than change
the broad boulevard empties, shops close early,
filling stations run out of fuel.
The last restaurant posts a menu of misspelled pies,
lists customers' names, warning:

BAD CHECKS.

Haunts me, says Jim,
so many unpaid ghosts.

The Confluence

Fort Defense, Illinois

Here was the clear Ohio water
in shore, sure enough, and outside
was the old regular Muddy!

Here is America's heartbeat:
two spinning rivers writhe in circles,
charge into the watery labyrinth:
another beat, another maddened run.

Here is America's torn body,
battered as the continent.
Here tectonic plates broke the earth,
shuddered plains, shook the river
until her waters ran backward.

Here lies the nation's sin:
mixture of blue northern currents
and mud-brown chattel;
no operatic chorus of Old Man River
can avert retribution. Huck and Jim,
tricked by fog and fear couldn't escape;
they missed the confluence.

Here Twain's pen stopped cold.

Mister, is that town Cairo?
If you want to know, go and find out.
If you stay here botherin' around me
for about half a minute longer,
you'll get something you won't want.

Here read the future as the human palm:
here the forests breathe bad air;
water's undrinkable; rubble chokes the channel.

43

Here the note falls due.
Here nature's nation, wounded,
proceeds without us.

The Prophecy

"Jim, do you smell rain?"
"No. I ain't no dog."

Prophecy Fulfilled

Approaching Dorena, Missouri

By noon, the green-black sky resembles
towboat smoke on the river; wiper blades
swipe silver-dollar raindrops, lacquer glass.

I look for the ferry boat slip to Kentucky,
an updraft suddenly lifts the rain, reveals
the naked Mississippi, oval blotches pelt
on wrinkled skin, shivers in wind-gusts up
from the south; the river vanishes in haze.

A pickup enters the passing lane, tires spray
the windows, see one red tail light, then two.
I recall our classmate, David, skidded in '66
through a VW window, dead at twenty-eight.
"He left first, he never had to fail," says Jim.

He lifts his foot from the pedal, wheels glide
on slippery black liquid.

Surface Tension

Whispers of rain cross
the river from Dorena to Hickman,
a soft wind muffles the ferry motor.
Water flat, ruffles with undercurrents.
We stand on deck
soaked by light rain,
sandbars hiding sinkholes.

The Loneliness of River Towns: I

South from Hickman, Kentucky

a pretty town perched on a handsome hill

The solitude of river towns,
storefronts broken; Dixie Theater closed,
last boat's a century gone,
creaking freight trains bound elsewhere.

No cafés, we eat with plastic forks
in a filling station, order bottles of Bud;
the elderly soft-voiced waitress apologizes,
"Ah just don't know anythin' 'bout beer."

The Loneliness of River Towns: II

Tiptonville, Tennessee

unchanging sameness of serenity,
repose, tranquility, lethargy, vacancy –
symbol of eternity

A 1941 lunch menu taped to the wall
in a second-hand shop,
two men wearing straw hats
laugh about the night
a tourist drove "clear through town"
into the brown stream;
the older one snaps a match
against his nail, lights a cigar,
laughs again,
"clear through."

The Loneliness of River Towns: III

Southern Missouri

looking very unwell,
otherwise unchanged

Another dusky Main Street:
red pickup stands at the town's stop sign,
driver flipping headlights on and off;
boys in lettered t-shirts
lay bikes near a curbside sign:

NOISE ORDINANCE
BOOM BOXES
STRICTLY ENFORCED
TURN IT DOWN

How does a kid escape? asks Jim
Will they ever see New Orleans?

Empty Stomachs

Entering Arkansas

Hot corn-pone from Arkansas –
  split it, butter it,
  close your eyes and enjoy

On the Great River Road,
we scout for four-letter solutions:

FOOD-EATS-CAFÉ

In shabby towns the storefronts offer

SMALL MOTOR REPAIRS

Black men stand among pyramids of bald tires,
bait and tackle shops, the used car lot;
I glance inside a beauty parlor furnished
with one mirror, a shelf of colors.

When it comes to food,
          crusty catfish, fried okra, biscuits, iced tea;

        Try it, and grieve for the angels
        for they have it not!

Strangers here, we're way past lunchtime,

        and I am so hungry
        to know…
        these strange marvels,
        these impossible things

No one gives us a bug's glance.

Gravity and the River

On the Memphis levee

The big river pours south
as gravity wraps around the moon –
no white water or rapid falls,
monotonous, steady flow.

Under blazing sun, where the high bridge attaches Arkansas to
       Tennessee,
blurred color streaks, 18-wheelers in a high speed chase;
autos blare, squeal rubber down the mid-city ramps.

Here the river's wider than a mile, stretches
from cotton fields to cobbled streets;
big waters born 800 miles above
rush downstream
toward bone-dry acres 400 miles below,
subvert the human scale.

We Don't Talk Much About Women

Two men
shy to talk about women we've loved
except ex-wives,
the way failed husbands regret
blows they gave
and received.

Later we take turns recalling
the ones who slipped away,
interludes, affairs, opportunities
found and lost.
We don't talk
much about women who love us,
afraid to show we're vulnerable.

Tennessee Typographical

Stop the car, Jim.
He circles back,
I copy the big sign,
white letters on black felt

THE CHURCH OF CHRIST STANDS
IN OPPOSITION TO SEXUAL PERVERSION,
UNGODLINESS & ALL SOUL CONDEMING SIN

"Can't spell a damn," says Jim.

The Unfortunate Incident

Helena, Arkansas

"Main Street of the Blues" – I'll tell you why,
Jim says: here ten years ago
I asked the oldest man I ever met
to tell a story he'd heard
from the oldest man *he'd* met:

Black sharecroppers at a nighttime meeting,
cabin surrounded by orange-tipped cigars.
Guns flashed; the wounded ran into the woods,
treed for days; hunters tossed the bodies
onto north-bound freights.

Now no one knows what Jim's talking about,
the "unfortunate incident" is gone;
Jim's just learned the oldest man
he ever met has died.

Secrets of Sand

We play in the sand,
    each covering his neighbor up
and times we make mud pastry. . .
        we do fairly wallow in the mud

Sand shimmers on the Arkansas levee,
birds flutter in a lidded sky,
circle back to cracked shore;
heat dries every desire.

"This weather's like Iraq":
Jim conjures the desert wind,
green trucks convoy his former students
through blizzards of brittle airborne grains.

One emails a term paper from Baghdad;
another home with medals, Mom so proud,
he's ashamed to tell her
he flattened five kids with a tank.

"He comes into my office and cries,"
says Jim. That boy
can only talk about sand.

Sunset on the River

Benoit, Mississippi

The last sunrays streak
the river skin; cicadas strum,
water bugs dance in tiny rings,
evening doves respond:

night songs haunt the hidden cove,
every living thing prepares
for hunted darkness,
except the river, continuing
without hunger.

Mississippian Mystery

Winterville Mounds

This ghost town of earthen crests,

> *domed and pinnacled mass,*
> *glimmering through a tinted,*
> *exquisite mist. . .a dozen*
> *shapely pyramids watched*
> *over ruined Memphis*

the old forest gone
a thousand years.

Ancient Mississippians hauled baskets
of soil, built flat-topped pyramids
clustered above oval plazas.

> *looking toward the verge*
> *of the landscape. . .over*
> *lines of century waves*

What did they do and why?
memory lost,
ransacked hills won't talk.

The Southern Shroud

Vicksburg, Mississippi

Wild kudzu devours the hills,
pea-green vines ascend
on every line that rises:
shrub, tree, signpost, power pole,
the wires that span from house to barn,
everything unsheltered
from the ravenous shroud.
Even the riverboat casinos insist
kudzu green
is the only color of the night.

Mound Dwellers

Vicksburg's National Military Park

the dying man gave me
a reproachful look. . .
this thing I have done
does not end with him

Suddenly, in the hot afternoon,
two underground black powder bombs
exploded (a stunned Confederate slave
blown over enemy lines to freedom).

Mound dwellers,
men buried among men;
or shot conventionally by minie bullets,
torn by shells at Champion's Hill,
Big Black River, Baker Creek Bridge;
merely measled
and pocked into hallucinatory fever –

We circle Illinois Temple,
classic square, granite and marble
crowned by a golden eagle,
thirty-six thousand names
in bronze.

Not Without Thy Wondrous Story
Illinois, Illinois
Can Be Writ the Nation's Glory
Illinois, Illinois

therefore,
Lincoln would say:
"The Father of Waters again
goes unvexed to the sea."

Steps in the Wilderness

Along the Natchez Trace

We search for signs in the woods,
faded footprints, a broken stick; I try
to picture the ones who've preceded us,
earlier selves. Where did we lose
the way?

Today there's no trace, no wilderness,
the forty-mile parkway barbered;
shady trees line smooth shoulders,
cucumber-green grass rolls into hayricks,
a monotonous ride; it's why children

fall asleep in the back seat,
adults speak softly of destinations.
We approach New Orleans, Jim and I,
retrace the map, pursue our mad descent,
the fear we had of renewal,
starting over.

We took a little room upstairs,
big beds on a balconied street;
a friend's Tampax spilled from my bag,
a smile lit Jim's face, dark eyes singing:
"Because I'm a southern gentleman,
I'll just surmise."

To the saloon, barmaids cooed and goosed,
Sugar Bowl boys dipped snuff, Jim bought
Bourbon and branch water, two by two;
we swaggered into noisy streets, shoved
to Jackson Square, the old general grabbing

his bucking horse; two-man brass band
blew The Saints; we edged through

61

a urine-smelling passageway,
pulled toward afternoon light, found
the levee, water wide, running.

> *Here they are! They've broke*
> *for the river! after 'em boys!*
> *And turn loose the dogs!*

Riverborne, two young men crossed
the stream, scent evaporates, hounds
scratch and howl along the shores,
a grisly sheriff mutters: "Gone."

Not even a smile was findable anywhere.

Perdition's what remains, being lost:
no mailbox, dental chart, no skeptical detective
chases the cold trail: Gone without trace,
we'd scarcely imagined
how far they recede in time.

Soon we'll touch the horse's tail,
stand where the river pours into sea;
we won't face each other, but turn
to allow an upriver glance, turn back
to shivered loss.

Visible Saints

Vidalia, Louisiana

betting on anything that turned up. . .
he can outjump any frog

Two dopes, we could become millionaires,
beat the loosest slots on the "Isle of Capri,"
where fortune flutters below the bluffs:
sparkling churches, sermons, prayers,
the second chance that comes at night,
Jesus riding a Black Jack to the perfect Ace.

lucky, uncommonly lucky. . .
ready and laying for a chance

A jingling gospel calls the reprobate to casino tent-camp:
speedboats slap the current, crawl past the jetty;
shuttle buses dip toward shore, autos flashing headlights.
At the threshold, men open-collared in tuxedos plant
cigarettes in bowls of sand; Afro women come in gowns;
a worker, lunch box tucked at the elbow, strides inside.

a frog so modest and straight fo'ward. . .
for all he was so gifted

Fearless before house rules, intelligent design,
players approach green felt tables, ritualistic,
lips in silent prayer, furtive kiss to the dice--
the bet, the roll: As they entered so they exit,
winners and losers equal, and next time for sure,
they'll dwell among God's chosen children.

bet on Parson Walker. . .the best exhorter. . .
all a frog wanted was education

Sunday morning we spot a white pimp Cadillac limo,
satellite antennae on the hood, two rectangle plaques
gleam in sunshine: CLERGY-PASTOR; the aged driver
emerges, leaning on a crooked cane, limps to his pulpit.
"Jim," I inquire: "You think the meek inherit the Earth?"
"This casino goes," he smirks, "the whole town's done."

Southern Pep Talk

WHERE THE SOUTH BEGINS

WHERE LIFE FEELS GOOD AGAIN

EXPECT A MIRACLE,
WORSHIP WITH US

GOD IS LOVE

I LOVE YOU GOD

GOD IS PRO-LIFE

WHO'S YOUR DADDY?

IN ALL THY WAYS
ACKNOWLEDGE HIM
AND HE SHALL
DIRECT THY PATH

THE STRENGTH OF THE LORD
IS THE STRENGTH TO BE UPRIGHT

THEREFORE HEAR THE COUNSEL
OF THE LORD

JESUS IS COMING SOON

THE WORKS OF THE FLESH
THE FRUIT OF THE SPIRIT
WHICH PORTRAYS YOUR LIFE?

PREVENT TOOTH DECAY
BRUSH UP ON YOUR BIBLE

JESUS IS HOPE

IS CHRIST RISEN IN YOU?

SIN, DEBT
JESUS PAYS
OR YOU DO

JESUS GOT'R DONE

THIS IS THE HOUSE
OF PRAYER. ALL IS WELCOME

NO BUMS

BIRTHPLACE OF
ROCK AND ROLL

BE STILL. . .
AND KNOW THAT I AM GOD

EXPERIENCE YOUR AMERICA

THE TRUE GOSPEL IS
PREACHED HERE

A CERTIFIED RETIREMENT CITY

ALONE YOU CAN'T
TOGETHER WE CAN

A MAIN STREET COMMUNITY

THE HOME OF
THE DOUBLE HEADED EAGLE

A CITY ON THE MOVE

COME AS OUR VISITOR

LEAVE AS OUR FAMILY

RED CARPET CITY OF THE SOUTH

JESUS IS A FRIEND
WHO WALKS IN
WHEN THE WORLD
HAS WALKED OUT

WE BUY AND SELL
EVERYTHING

WALMART ISN'T THE ONLY
SAVING PLACE

FIRE FIGHTERS RESCUE
ONLY JESUS SAVES

IF GOD IS YOUR CO-PILOT
SWAP SEATS

HIGH WATER POSSIBLE

GOD IS IN CONTROL
HE CALMS THE WATERS

GOOSE CAPITAL OF THE WORLD

WELCOME HOME
PFC CLINT OLIVER

Reprieve

Natchez, Mississippi

Einstein's right, time bends
toward mass, quickened
by years, but crawls
into caves of echoed voices.

We began, Mississippi slept
in bed, no point to the trip
but its possibility. Now we know
more: this time's the last time.

We're not ready for the end;
advance toward a throng
gathered in a motel lobby, staring at TV,
rolling headlines forecast the day:

BRACING FOR KATRINA!
EVACUATE NEW ORLEANS

The city's closed! No entry!
Quickly we calculate the odds:
let's go south, ride out the storm
and – but there is no and. . . .

And uncontrollable as hurricane rain
drenches the land, our fear evaporates:
what Jim and I know, not frustration
but deliverance, reprieve.

Turn Upriver

Toward St. Louis

We do what tens of thousands must, head North;
our talk's dispirited as surrounding acres
of chopped cotton, dull-colored barns,
toppled fences, rusty trailers.

We pass prison towns, warning of hitchhikers;
at Ken's Crossroads, encounter sullen hospitality.
Outside white deputies watch an orange-clad trustee
pump gas; a cemetery lines the road through town.

Isolated Waterproof, miles from the moving river,
Main Street domino of ruin, only churches open.
Near Tallulah, we follow dirt roads to the riverfront,
odor of ragweed, toasted yellow-tipped grass.

In a Memphis lobby, Carib-accented man in turquoise
holds a daughter's small hand, her pink t-shirt flashes
hearts. He's lost "everything else." "You know
what matters," I blurt, as if I do; we've lost nothing,

except the saccharine symmetry of a happy ending.
Will we ever see New Orleans? Never as it was.
In St. Louis, we'll talk of failure, feel the grace
of not going somewhere special for the last time.

Postscript to a Flood

Noah and his family were saved –
if that could be called an advantage

Trapped by insistent coverage,
aerial views of heroic rescue,
failure, the waters rising,

a woman in pale nightgown, hair
soaked, wails on a rooftop,
calls for her boy. As rain falls

we get newsroom advice: Stock Up
on Matches, Name Tag Your Children –
as if, says Jim, the river will stop.

From elongated tail to slippery tongue:
nothing but that frail breastwork of earth
between the people and devastation.

Skin insulates the body, the puncture
bleeds. Dark waters dissolve,
submerge, the earth sinks.

This river's a planetary seam,
doesn't reason, think, want.
What are two people to a river?

The same as two thousand, two billion:
Mississippi is everything they are not;
the river outlives every desire.

Immortality's a human misunderstanding:
when I say goodbye to Jim at the airport,
we know the continent can't last forever.

Endnotes

Page 3   *recognized him at once*: *Mark Twain's Own Autobiography: The Chapters from the North American Review*, edited by Michael J. Kiskis (Madison, Wisconsin, 1990), pp. 54-55.

Page 4   *but Jim said: Adventures of Huckleberry Finn* (Berkeley, California, 2002), p. 63.

Page 5   *the "point" above*: *Life on the Mississippi* (New York, 2000), p. 20.

Page 6   *The city. . .greatly changed*: *Life on the Mississippi*, p. 107.

Page 8   *apple roasting. . .sizzling*: *Mark Twain's Own Autobiography*, p. 121.

Page 9   *We-no-na ran to its summit*: *Life on the Mississippi*, pp. 265-66.

Page 11   *A choice town*: *Life on the Mississippi*, p. 262.

Page 14   *tranquil and reposeful*: *Life on the Mississippi*, p. 261.

Page 16   *it might be the spirits*: *The Adventures of Tom Sawyer* (New York, 2001), p. 70.

Page 20   *ground-shaking, thunder-crashes*: *Life on the Mississippi*, p. 166.

               Since Grant has whipped: William S. McFeely, *Grant: A Biography* (New York, 1981), p. 237.

Page 26   *Mamma, what's it all for?*: *Mark Twain's Own Autobiography*, p. 28.

Page 28   *new houses—saw. . .plainly*: Life on the Mississippi, p. 237.

Page 31   *swinging signs creaked*: The Tragedy of Pudd'nhead Wilson (New York, 1964), p. 22; *Life on the Mississippi,* p. 20.

Page 32   *comrades and yet not comrades*: Quoted in Mark Perry Grant and Twain: The Story of an American Friendship (New York, 2004), p. 215.

Page 33   *vague general knowledge*: Life on the Mississippi, p. 22

               domes and steeples: Mark Twain and Charles Dudley Warner, *The Gilded Age* (Seattle, 1968), pp. 31, 90.

Page 35   *pavements. . .bad*: Life on the Mississippi, p. 109.

Page 40   *easily rememerable*: Life on the Mississippi, p. 118.

Page 41   *Brisk town*: Life on the Mississippi, p. 120.

Page 43   *Here was the clear Ohio*: Huckleberry Finn, p. 129.

Page 48   *a pretty town*: Life on the Mississippi, p. 120.

Page 49   *unchanging sameness*: Life on the Mississippi, p. 126.

Page 50   *looking very unwell*: Life on the Mississippi, p. 125.

Page 51   *Hot corn-pone*: No. 44, the Mysterious Stranger (Berkeley, Calif., 1982), pp. 112-13.

Page 56   *We play*: The Prince and the Pauper (New York, n.d.), p. 11.

Page 58   *domed and pinnacled mass*: *The Innocents Abroad or the New Pilgrim's Prayer* (New York, 1966), pp. 453, 457-58.

Page 60   *the dying man*: "The Private History of a Campaign that Failed," *The Signet Classic Book of Mark Twain's Short Stories* (New York, 1985), p. 282.
Not Without Thy Wondrous Story: Illinois State Song, Words by Charles Chamberlin (1841-1894).

Page 62   *Here they are!*: *Huckleberry Finn*, p. 346.

Page 62   *Not even a smile*: "The Man that Corrupted Hadleyburg," *Signet Book of Short Stories*, p. 412.

Page 63   *betting on anything*: "The Notorious Jumping Frog of Calaveras County," *Signet Book of Short Stories*, p. 2.

Page 70   *Noah and his family*: *Letters from the Earth*, edited by Bernard DeVoto (New York, 1974), p. 34.

                     nothing but that frail breastwork: *Life on the Mississippi*, p. 188.

AUTHOR

Peter Neil Carroll, born in New York City in 1943, discovered the Mississippi River as a history teacher in Minnesota and frequently visited the Delta region from southern Missouri to New Orleans. He has written and edited numerous books, including the memoir *Keeping Time: Memory, Nostalgia, & the Art of History*. He has taught creative writing at the University of San Francisco, hosted *"Booktalk"* on Pacifica Radio, and edited the *San Francisco Review of Books*. He lives in Belmont, California with the writer Jeannette Ferrary.